Water Stone Sky

My heart is awed within me when I think
Of the great miracle that still goes on,
In silence, round me — the perpetual work
Of thy creation, finished, yet renewed Forever.

    Bryant, "A Forest Hymn"

Water Stone Sky

A Pictorial Essay on Lake Powell
Second Edition

Stanley L. Welsh and
Catherine Ann Toft

Brigham Young University Press
Provo, Utah

Library of Congress Cataloging in Publication Data

Welsh, Stanley L
 Water, stone, sky.

 1. Powell, Lake—Pictorial works. I. Toft, Catherine
Ann, 1950-   joint author. II. Title.
GB1625.U8W44   1976   551.4'82'097925   75-45003
ISBN 0-8425-1016-8

Library of Congress Catalog Card Number: 75-45003
International Standard Book Number: 0-8425-1016-8
© 1976 Brigham Young University Press. All rights reserved
New, revised, enlarged edition
First edition © 1974 Brigham Young University Press
Brigham Young University Press, Provo, Utah 84602
Printed in the United States of America
76 10M 16515

Contents

Prologue xi

Preface xiii

Introduction 1

The Canyon 9

The Region 13

The Stone 17

Reflections 21

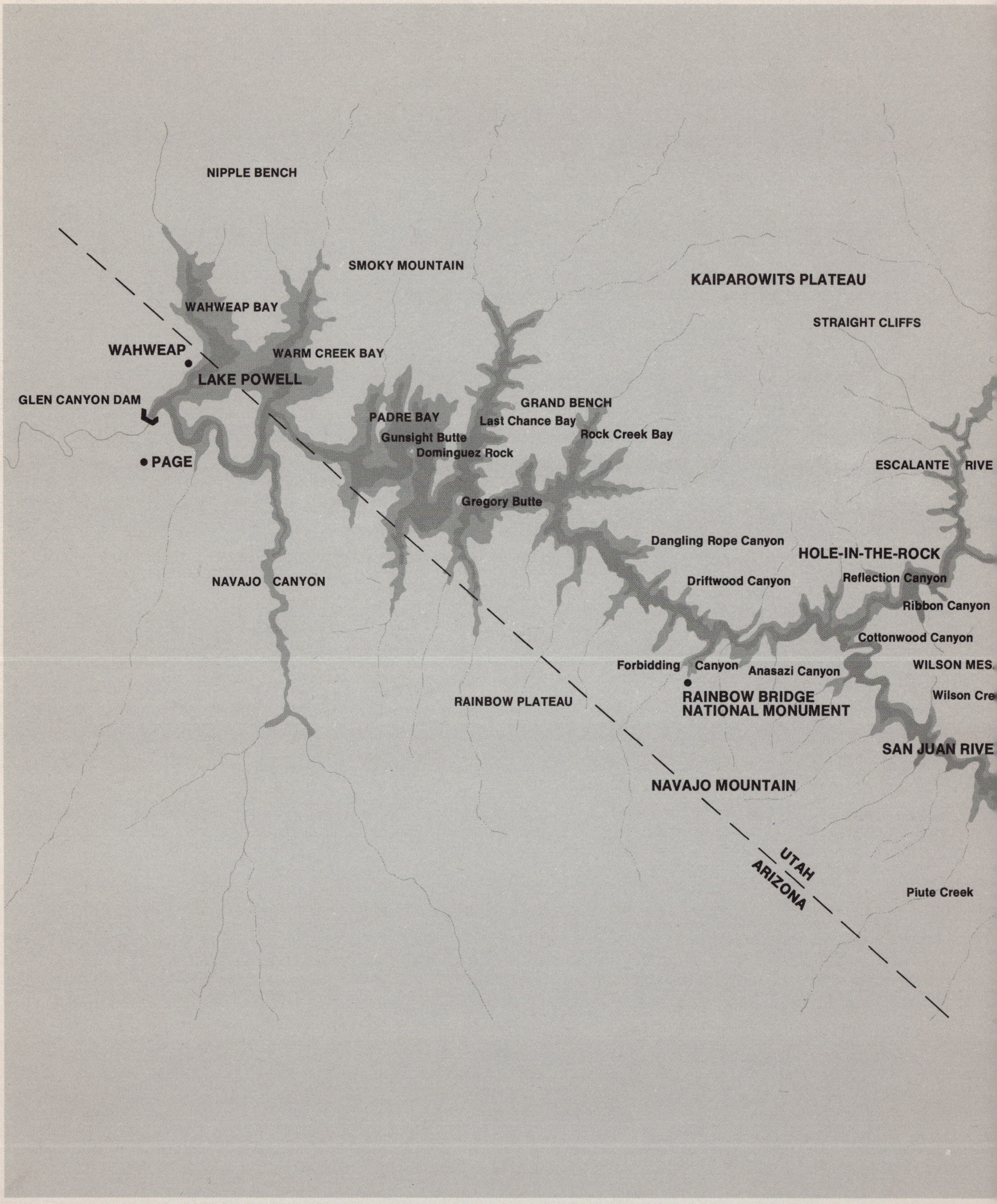

NIPPLE BENCH

SMOKY MOUNTAIN

KAIPAROWITS PLATEAU

WAHWEAP BAY

STRAIGHT CLIFFS

WAHWEAP
LAKE POWELL
WARM CREEK BAY

GLEN CANYON DAM

GRAND BENCH
PADRE BAY Last Chance Bay
Gunsight Butte Rock Creek Bay
Dominguez Rock

PAGE

ESCALANTE RIVE

Gregory Butte

Dangling Rope Canyon

NAVAJO CANYON

HOLE-IN-THE-ROCK

Driftwood Canyon Reflection Canyon

Ribbon Canyon

Cottonwood Canyon

Forbidding Canyon Anasazi Canyon WILSON MES.

RAINBOW BRIDGE
NATIONAL MONUMENT

RAINBOW PLATEAU

Wilson Cre

SAN JUAN RIVE

NAVAJO MOUNTAIN

UTAH
ARIZONA

Piute Creek

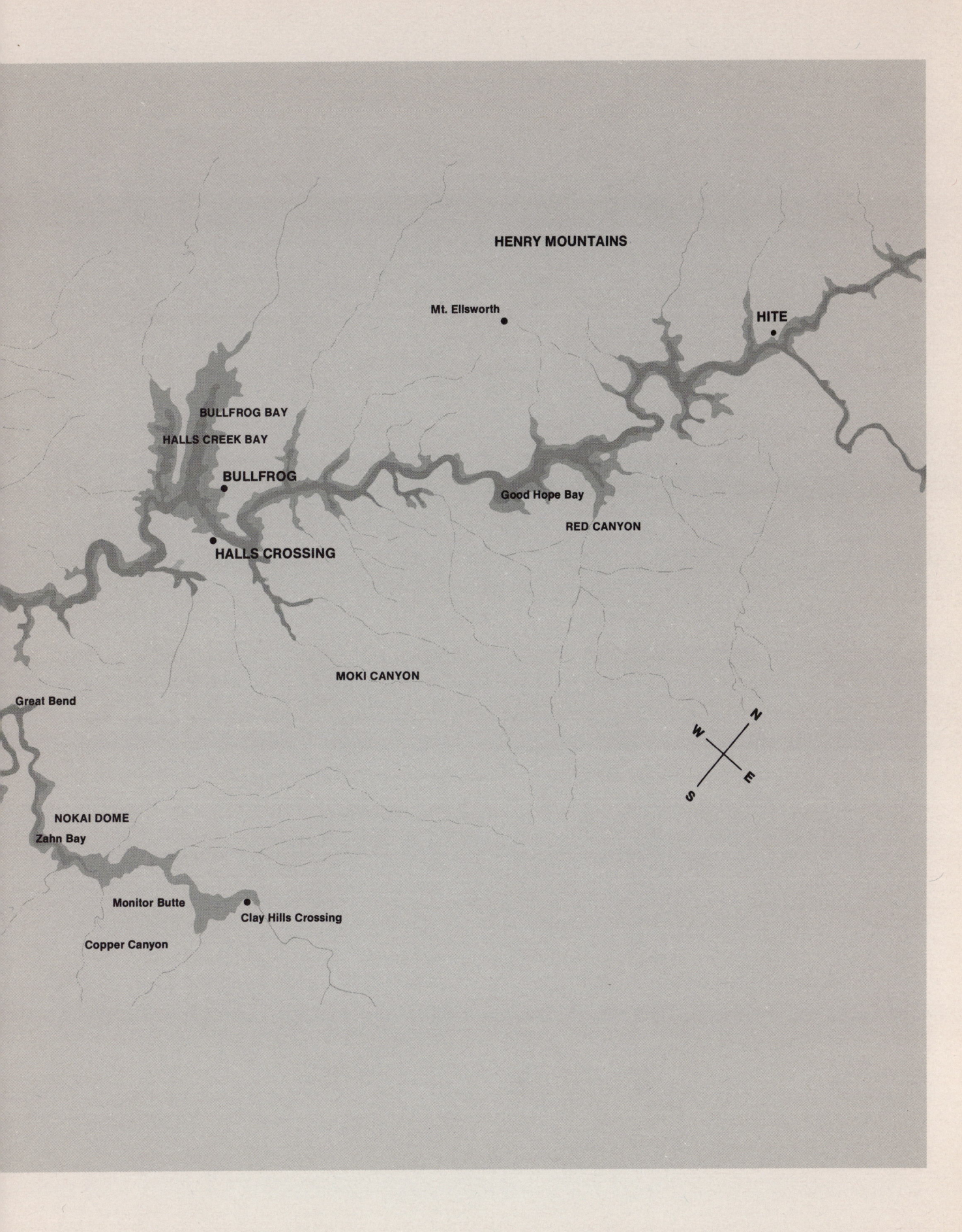

Prologue

Much water has flowed through the penstocks at Glen Canyon Dam since we began the research leading to the first edition of *Water, Stone, Sky*. Additionally, the difference between the water passing through the gates of the dam and that which entered the lake from upstream has led to an increase of almost a hundred feet in the level of Lake Powell. Marginal land along the lake has been inundated as the trapped waters have accumulated saltatorially with annual runoff from the snowpack high in the basins of the Colorado drainage system. Now we mourn the loss of that segment of the remainder of Glen Canyon that we came to know so well.

    Smoothly cleft walls of stone, jagged overhanging cliffs, gently sloping shelves of rock, dainty and graceful plants of maidenhair fern, western redbud, and cardinal flower have all given way to the relentless waters. Hanging gardens, containing their relics of past life, lie submerged beneath the lake surface, their floras reduced or extinct. Plant species at the margin of their range in Glen Canyon have ceased to exist as their unique habitats have been lost to the lake.

    What is the loss? — The knowledge that one more place wherein man could find peace of mind has ceased to exist, except in the subconsciousness and consciousness of those who experienced it. Future generations will not be able to find that place or to experience it. The present generation has made a value judgment that the short-term benefits of Glen Canyon Dam and Lake Powell are worth the trade-off. Are they?

Preface

To the First Edition

There are those who mourn the passing of Glen Canyon of the Colorado River — "the place no one knew." Burying the glens and alcoves, the grottos and narrow defiles — all temples of nature — the blue-black waters of Lake Powell rise more than 400 feet in the narrow inner gorge. Some of us never saw "the place no one knew," but we, too, can regret its passing. Even as we float on the lake's serene waters and watch the interplay of light on its reflective surface mirroring the pink sandstone, we think of the drowned canyon and its ghosts of desert gardens, hidden for an eternity by the massive depths. Even more, we think of the leashed river, the tempestuous Colorado, which embodied the violence of this harsh land, now a prisoner in the canyon of its own carving, its swift waters dissipated in the calm depths of the lake.

Lake Powell, like the land along it, is a paradox. At the same time that its waters have buried a canyonland, stream bottoms, and other wonders, it has displayed a new world previously inaccessible to mankind. Skimming over its waters, we can discover an entirely different world than could such early explorers as John Wesley Powell. Some hundreds of feet above the canyon bottom, we can glide along cliff faces where Powell would never have imagined a man could ever reach. Alcoves, shelves, and rocky ledges are now accessible, forbidden before to the human race by their impossible positions along a canyon wall.

Stepping over a cliff, a move which a decade ago would have meant death, now immerses us in the placid waters of an emerald pool. A swimming human form rippling the surface of the lake occupies a position previously restricted to flying things.

Mostly the lake fills only the narrow inner gorge. Above its waters rises a land of superb sandstone cliffs, a desert country both harsh and beautiful. Perhaps there is not as much of this country as there once was — some elements are missing — but the remaining land beyond the water's edge stands in its superb, ethereal, natural glory. Reflected in the lake and stretching from it in the hazy distance is the slickrock country, undaunted by the brief instant since the lake was born — still "a place no one knows."

We dedicate this book to the beauty of Lake Powell, to an understanding of the features which bound its shores, and to a knowledge of the processes which produced this splendid region. Its intent is to record, in a small way, a portion of the slickrock country along Glen Canyon as it now exists and as much of it existed in the ages before the land felt the presence of the modern world. Let us not mourn for Glen Canyon so much that our eyes are closed to the marvels of this rugged canyon country, marvels reflected in the exotic waters of an ephemeral lake. We should well mourn, however, if some future generation should accuse us of walking through this great land with eyes closed, allowing it to remain "the place no one knew."

Introduction

The region around Glen Canyon has traditionally been one of the most remote and most inaccessible in Utah and Arizona. Despite this fact, the canyon and its surroundings were penetrated very early by explorers preceding the period of the great westward migration. During 1776, the year of the founding of our nation, Fathers Silvestre Velez de Escalante and Francisco Atanacio Dominguez, Spanish priests, crossed Glen Canyon after they failed to reach California while traveling with a party "to discover a route from the Presidio at Santa Fe, New Mexico, to Monterey in northern California."

It was late in the season. Autumn had come, and trails were difficult to find. The party searched for a place where they could reach the river, deep in its protective canyon. According to historians, on October 26, 1776, the expedition reached the river, probably at the site of Lee's Ferry. Here they constructed rafts, but since the water was very deep and poles cut for the purpose of propelling the rafts would not reach bottom, the attempt to cross failed. Three days later Escalante recorded in his diary a statement which indicates something of the condition of the expedition: "Not knowing when we would be able to leave this place, and having already eaten up the meat of the first horse, the pine kernals [sic], and the other provisions we had brought, we ordered another horse killed."

From their camp of October 29, Escalante, Dominguez, and party climbed to the escarpment which borders the lower end of Glen Canyon and attempted to find another approach to the river. Through Wahweap, Warm Creek, and Gunsight Butte canyons they searched in bewilderment and awe in this vast technicolor land for a downward route. They camped one night near the base of Romana Mesa; here, it rained during the night, and in the morning it was very cold.

Near Gunsight Butte they found an Indian trail winding through a narrow defile and leading into a deep gorge carved into the massive Navajo Sandstone. In one place the way was sufficiently precipitous that the horses could not descend, even though the men were walking and leading them. Steps were cut into the stone with an ax for a few yards, and the party continued. Finally, on November 7, 1776, in a wild, remote, and desolate region, they found a place where the river ran very wide, where Indians had crossed since time immemorial. This place was later designated as "El Vado de los Padres," or Crossing of the Fathers.

The river was very broad and ran not too swiftly at the ford so that the men and their animals were able to wade it without swimming. The journey beyond the river was almost as difficult as that in reaching it, but the expedition finally arrived at Santa Fe on New Year's Day of 1777.

Almost a century later, on August 3, 1869, John Wesley Powell's party, in boats deep within the canyon, reached the point where Escalante and Dominguez had crossed the Colorado River. Powell recorded a description of the crossing place in his journal:

A little stream comes down through a very narrow side canyon [Padre Canyon] from the west. It was down this that he [Escalante] came and our boats are lying at the point where the ford crosses. A well beaten Indian trail is seen here yet. Between the cliff and the river there is a little meadow. The ashes of many camp fires are seen, and the bones of numbers of cattle are bleaching on the grass.

Powell had entered Glen Canyon several days before, on the morning of July 29, 1869, after a difficult journey through Cataract Canyon which is continuous with Glen Canyon to the north. The single sentence: "We enter a canyon today, with low, red walls," introduces the reader of Powell's diary to an account of Glen Canyon. Powell and his men were to leave the canyon at the present site of Lee's Ferry on the evening of August 4, 1869.

So it was that Powell spent almost one week in the canyon which he named after one of the features from within the rock-bound confines of the gorge: "On the walls, and back many miles into the country, a number of monument-shaped buttes are observed. So we have here a curious ensemble of wonderful features — carved walls, royal arches, glens, alcove gulches, mounds, and monuments. From which of these shall we select a name? We decided to call it Glen Canyon."

Descriptions of the canyon by Powell are among the very best written about this vast region. The record of the canyon for August 3, 1869, is typical:

The features of the canyon are greatly diversified. Still vertical walls at times. These are usually found to stand above great curves. The river, sweeping around these bends, undermines the cliffs in places.

Sometimes the rocks are overhanging; in other curves curious narrow glens are found. Through these we climb, by a rough stairway, perhaps several hundred feet, to where a spring bursts out from under an overhanging cliff and where cottonwoods and willows stand, while along the curves of the brooklet oaks grow, and other rich vegetation is seen, in marked contrast to the general appearance of naked rock. We call these Oak Glens.

Apparent barrenness along the great canyon is deceiving, for the land supports an abundance of living things both plant and animal. The plants of the arid lands are widely and irregularly spaced, with much bare ground between. Also, because of their dark gray to gray-green color, the plants tend to blend with the background. The only really green places occur along the water courses and around seeps and springs. Here, there is an abundance of living things, supported by life-giving water, usually in short supply away from the edge of these perpetually wet places.

Powell and his men suffered from the monotony of their food, which deteriorated in quality and diminished in quantity each day. However, a brief respite occurred on July 27, 1869, in Cataract Canyon:

Late in the afternoon we pass to the left around a sharp point . . ., and discover a flock of mountain sheep on the rocks more than a hundred feet above us. We land quickly out of sight, and away go all the hunters with their guns, for the sheep have not discovered us. Soon we hear firing. . . . One sheep has been killed, and two of the men are still pursuing them. In a few minutes we hear firing again, and the next moment down came the flock clattering over the rocks within 20 yards of us. One of the hunters seizes his gun and brings a second sheep down, and the next minute the remainder of the flock is lost behind the rocks. . . . We lash our prizes to the deck of one of the boats and go on for a short distance; but fresh meat is too tempting for us, and we stop early to have a feast. And a feast it is. Two fine young sheep. We care not for bread or beans or dried apples tonight; coffee and mutton are all we ask.

Mountain sheep still are found along the plateaus and canyons bordering Glen Canyon, mainly eastward on Wilson Mesa. The sighting of a desert bighorn is reason for celebration because their numbers have dwindled since Powell's time. Deer browse on vegetation in the side canyons, where beaver still gnaw the cottonwood trees and build small dams across the tiny streams. Skunk, gray fox, coyote, and badger are the most common carnivores; but on the plateaus and in canyons at higher elevations cougars still pursue deer and other game.

Indians had inhabited Glen Canyon for centuries before Powell floated through its dark reaches. Evidence of the earlier presence of Indians is found in such items as a bit of corrugated jar near a permanent pool in an alcove and arrowheads and chipped fragments of chert along the mesas and shelves near the canyon. Small dwellings with T-shaped doors, tucked neatly into alcoves, mostly those which face toward the south, give testimony of a more permanent occupation. Civilization penetrated into the region with the advent of an agricultural Indian society dependent on corn, beans, and squash.

That civilization flourished for half a millennium and then retreated southward before Columbus discovered America. The land then served as a hunting ground for the wandering peoples who lived in a meager way in this difficult land.

Nearly a decade after Powell had traversed Glen Canyon, in the autumn of 1879, another party gathered alongside this barrier. The expedition became known as the Hole-in-the-Rock party. They are referred to again later in this book, but they must be mentioned here also. To that group, Glen Canyon was simply a mighty barrier, an obstacle, to be crossed at a price. The crossing was a means to an end, "a short cut," a way to reach a goal which was eastward along the San Juan River. That the Hole-in-the-Rock party was successful is a tribute to the endurance, cooperation, and zeal of the people in the expedition. And the story of their task is an example of people doing their very best under conditions of hardship and of sharing a common cause. Their backs were against a wall; it had snowed in the mountains behind them, closing the passes, and they had to arrive along the San Juan River before the spring planting season.

Powell and his men were similarly united by the hardship of their journey. In 1895, Powell wrote a preface to his *Canyons of the Colorado.* He recognized the men who had accompanied him and paid tribute to them:

Many years have passed since the exploration, and those who were boys with me are — ah, most of them are dead, and the living are gray with age. Their bronzed, hardy, brave faces come before me as they appeared in the vigor of life; their lithe but powerful forms seem to move around me; and the memory of the men and their heroic deeds, the men and their generous acts, overwhelms me with a joy that seems almost a grief, for it starts a fountain of tears. I was a maimed man; my right arm was gone; and these brave men, these good men, never forgot it. In every danger my safety was their first care, and in every waking hour some kind of service was rendered me, and they transfigured my misfortune into a boon. To you — J. C. Sumner, William H. Dunn, W. H. Powell, G. Y. Bradley, O. G. Howland, Seneca Howland, Frank Goodman, W. R. Hawkins, and Andrew Hall — my noble and generous companions, dead and alive, I dedicate this book.

Even before Powell launched his expedition at Green River, Wyoming, on May 24, 1869, the region on the west side of Glen Canyon had been visited by white men on several occasions. Stockmen were grazing livestock — cattle, horses, and sheep — in the vicinity. Settlements had been established along the Escalante and the Dirty Devil rivers. But Powell made the region known in a scientific way by plotting the location of prominent features and by mapping the region.

Dreamers and schemers later attempted to utilize resources from the great canyon for personal gain, mostly failing because of low returns and high expenditures of time and energy.

Travelers utilized the canyon for a retreat, a place of solace, wherein their souls could be renewed, where, because of privation, physical comfort did not have to come first, where timeless scenes were painted in unbelievable reds, browns, and blacks, and where forms of rock, softly rounded or sheer and smooth, glided past hour after hour in silent grandeur. It was, for them, a place of peace and restoration.

But civilization has caught up with this land which was previously considered to be almost worthless, and a great plug was placed within the inner gorge at a place where a beehive-shaped rock marks the west rim of Glen Canyon a few miles upstream from Powell's camp of the night of August 4, 1869.

Glen Canyon Dam is a monument to modern technology. Constructed at tremendous cost, the dam effectively stopped the flow of the river and turned the inner gorge of the canyon into a huge lake, named to honor the memory of John Wesley Powell.

The lake is an anomaly in an arid land. The loss of water by evaporation is tremendous, and an additional measure flows into the sandstone walls of its irregular basin. Silt from the Colorado and its tributaries falls out as the streams enter the quiet waters of the lake, and the basin has already begun to shrink by the volume of silt it contains. The life of any lake is short, depending as it does on the size of the basin and on the nature of the waters which enter it. The life of Lake Powell is limited to a few decades, perhaps a century or two, but assuredly the lake will fill with sediment. The gorge itself is mute testimony that a volume of rock equal to its size was excavated by the river, and now from upstream come the silts of ages, flowing in the relentless waters.

The Canyon

Not all of the rugged and beautiful land lies beneath the surface of Lake Powell. The buried inner gorge, magnificent though it undoubtedly was, represents only a small portion of the canyon system of the Colorado River. Above the surface of the lake, along its shores, there is a land of superb technicolor geology with no imposing blanket of vegetation to mask it. On the whole, the shores are barren — often slickrock; more rarely a sandy beach occurs, but bare rock dominates. In few places of the world is the geology more spectacular. Here, red, pink, and white rocks abound, though elsewhere they are a rarity.

At first sight the landscape seems almost homogeneous. The cliffs and talus slopes are bare and seem almost monotone, but a trip along Lake Powell affords the chance of a trip through time, along a cross-section of a portion of the history of the earth. Many layers of rock — sandstone, siltstone, and mudstone — are present, each unique in color, texture, composition, history, and age. Yet the sequence is an orderly one. The strata appear in the same order wherever they occur, and they change gradually from place to place. Cross-bedded sands give way to bedded ones, whites and buffs to reds.

Rock layers in the vicinity of Lake Powell, in the lower reaches of the Green and the former Grand rivers and along the massive Colorado River canyon formed at their confluence, are a series of alternating layers of differing thicknesses of mud or silt and sandstones laid down mainly in the Mesozoic era. Traces of Paleozoic rocks lie in the bottom of the gorge. Cenozoic rocks cap the highest plateaus of the great outer canyon system. The Green, Grand, San Juan, and Colorado rivers and all of their dendritic tributaries have cut a series of supercanyons, and in portions of two of these canyons lies Lake Powell.

High on alpine ridges of the Continental Divide, to the east and to the north, these rivers have humble beginnings as crystal clear brooklets trickling from melting snow fields. From the Green River lakes of the Wind River Mountains in Wyoming comes the Green River, from the north through the towns named Green River in both Wyoming and Utah. The Colorado, or Grand River, as it should be known, is born in Rocky Mountain National Park to the northeast, where the water from high peaks collects into Grand Lake. From there it flows as a modest mountain stream, growing until it meets the Green River deep within the canyon south of Island-in-the-Sky in Canyonlands National Park. Here the two mighty rivers, the Green and the Grand, combine to form the greatest river of the region, the Colorado. Southward, along the northern side of the magnificent Navajo Mountain, the San Juan River joins the Colorado, coming from Wolf Creek Pass in the San Juan Mountains of southern Colorado, where its headwaters adjoin those of the Rio Grande, a great river which flows southeastward to the Gulf of Mexico.

A canyon such as that of the Colorado is much more than just the narrow inner gorge, which, with its dark reaches and troubled waters, forms perhaps the most intriguing portion. Eons of time have passed since the first water and silt from the juvenile Colorado River reached the sea. Its course finally became entrenched into the younger overlying formations. The tributaries cut laterally away from the main course, causing the retreat of those primeval canyon walls, and the first great series of cliffs were formed above the growing river. The retreat of phalanx upon phalanx of cliffs has been underway since that time. The canyon itself is evidence of its great antiquity.

Alternation of harder layers of sandstone with softer layers of mud and siltstone has allowed this grand-scale canyon formation. The mud and siltstones are softer than the sandstones and erode more rapidly. The more rapid rate of erosion produces undercutting and causes the collapse of the resistant sandstone layers above, which fall away in massive slabs, often breaking away along joint systems within the cliff. Where joint systems are not present, the slabs break from the cliffs by means of conchoidal fracture, resulting in the formation of vast fan-shaped scars which take upon themselves the appearance of burnished metal after long periods of time. The slabs of sandstone break in falling, and for a time they protect the angular slope of the softer underlying stratum. Regardless of the size of the slabs, however, they do not long remain. The angular boulders form only a thin mantle which is swept away a grain of sand at a time, as if the natural processes of weathering were loath to keep a house unclean — were loath to slow the process of the renewal of the earth. A boulder on a slope is destined to be unevenly deposited over a vast area of some future strata.

The fresh, bright faces of rock exposed as the slabs fall away change in time as they are affected by water, wind, sunlight, and changes in temperature.

Stripes of red water-washed sand and of blackish carbonaceous materials overlie desert varnish. These together merely ornament the patterned walls, and their basic design results from the nature of the cleavage of the rock.

Resulting from all these processes is a series of mosaic panoramas, from which one, limited only by the depth and breadth of his imagination, can create scenes. The size of the scenes in sandstone varies with the shape and size of the canyon walls. In places, unbroken tapestries are continuous along the great curves of stone above the meanders of the river and its tributaries. In other sites, the mosaic ornamentation covers only a small area: a portion of an alcove or a gently curving wall. No two sections of a panorama are alike, and all scenes change in quality as light and shadows play about the summits and depths of the great canyon system. These tapestried walls require long periods of time for the ornamentation to reach some magnificent climax, and timeless as they appear, the length of their existence is not great.

Even the most splendid scenes fall, slab by slab, and the timeless painter again adorns the fresh canvas. The processes of nature are resolute in marking the landscape with scenes of magnificence.

The Region

Lake Powell is situated near the south end of the Upper Colorado basin. The portion of the basin considered here is bounded on the north by the Tavaputs Plateau, where its southern escarpment comprises the Book, Brown, and Roan cliffs north of Price and Green River, Utah, and Grand Junction, Colorado. Surrounding the colorful middle portion of the basin are the massive Cretaceous cliffs of the Mesa Verde group of formations. On top of these are the Cenozoic formations, and these together make up the phalanx of cliffs, in places more than 100 miles wide, of the outer canyon of the Colorado. From between their bases erosion has removed uncounted thousands of cubic miles of material, grain by grain. The entire basin is a stage where the history of unending time has been played and will continue to be played.

Thrusting up through this series of sedimentary strata came fluid magmas, melting and lifting the formations, separating them and penetrating between them, not in one place, but in four. Resulting from the action of these volcanic intrusives are the islandlike ranges called LaSal, Henry, Abajo, and Navajo. On their flanks are canyons with streams carrying away both the solidified volcanic materials and the remnants of the sedimentary formations which extend fingerlike up their slopes.

In some places other kinds of plastic bodies also moved upwards. Large accumulations of salt had been buried deep within the earth, trapped when ancient salt seas evaporated and were overlaid by silt. Under tremendous pressure, masses of salt react as fluids. Flowing together they seek to rise upward, breaking through the seemingly impenetrable rock layers. Moving towards the surface, some of these salt accumulations finally were broached by the great river, and the salt was pirated downstream into the sea. The void left by the vanished salt did not persist. The unsupported formations settled as the salt was extracted, resulting in the formation of valleys such as Paradox, Spanish, Castle, and Salt, as well as Needles, Doll House, and Upheaval Dome.

Weathering does not occur at the same rate at all places. The region has received its name, Plateau Province, in recognition of its flat-topped monuments to time and to differential erosion. Mesas, buttes, spires — in fact all monoliths — are mere relicts of formations at the edges of the great canyon. Kaiparowits Plateau, Mesa Verde, Island-in-the-Sky,

Black Mesa, and Beckwith Plateau represent such remnants, and smaller features abound.

The age of the surface features is not necessarily the same because the retreat of cliffs exhibits the older underlying formations and because within the earth, forces are at play which have caused the strata to warp and to strain, to bulge and to fracture. Some regions have been warped upward and others downward. These changes affect the rate of erosion and display formations along some of the tributaries of the river — formations which can be seen elsewhere only within the deepest portions of the inner gorge.

Along the margins of the vast inner gorge, especially where the land alongside is of low relief, are terraces of water-washed gravels, sands, and clays. These were formed ages ago when the river was cutting at a higher level. The cobble is often flattened, with rounded edges, evidence that it has traveled far. Some of it had its origin in mountain ranges far to the east and north. Now the terraces are perched high above the level of the stream which deposited them.

Scenery, as we see it here, is the result of its history. Its beauty and grandeur reflect the timeless forces of nature in all their vast array. Man can only interpret and hope to understand that beauty.

The Stone

Northward from Lake Powell's southern end stands the escarpment of the Kaiparowits Plateau. Capping the plateau are the formations which comprise the Mesa Verde Group. The main strata of this group, visible along the higher portions of the plateau, are the Wahweap and Straight Cliffs formations, consisting of sandstones alternating with silts and muds which were formed as a series of barrier islands in warm seas of the Cretaceous. Quantities of coal are present within the Straight Cliffs Formation.

Beneath the strata of the Mesa Verde Group is the Tropic Shale which is transitional eastward with the extensive and very thick Mancos Shale. Both shales are very poorly cemented, and they weather quickly into gray clay. The surface of this clay is often marked by white encrustations of salts and is seldom obscured by the widely spaced plants.

Tropic Shale is a crumbly mass of magnificent colors dictated by the oxidation of its iron, mostly yellows and grays blending imperceptibly except where they are cut by some erosional channel; there in bold contrast, black stands out against yellow — soft, rounded, sensuous forms against a backdrop of cliffs and sky.

Bases of the Tropic Shale rest upon the thinnish Cretaceous Dakota Formation, also displaying thin layers of coal. The Dakota is seldom as much as fifty feet thick. From the lake the Dakota Formation is seldom visible. The Dakota is situated atop the coarse sandstone of the Morrison Formation or, where the Morrison is missing, directly atop the cliff-forming Entrada Sandstone. The Morrison Formation forms the stone caprock of the mesas and plateaus east from Warm Creek. The Entrada Sandstone is a thick and massive layer that is closely stratified in its upper members and cross-bedded in its lower portion. The cross-bedded part consists of ancient sand dunes now frozen in stone.

The Entrada Sandstone varies from chalky white with shades of rusty brown on its weathered surfaces north of Wahweap Bay to orange-red at Rock Creek. Between Wahweap and Rock Creek the chalky sandstone changes color, with tongues of white sandstone extending eastward for some distance along the formation. The smoothly rounded, hole-pocked, orange-red cliffs touching water's edge in Padre, Last Chance, and Rock Creek bays are Entrada Sandstone. The massive monoliths south and north of Padre Bay, including Leche-e Rock, Tower Butte, Gunsight Butte, and Gregory Butte, are sculpted in the Entrada.

The Entrada lies atop a thin layer of gypsiferous, red mudstone which represents the Carmel Formation in this region. The Carmel is frequently obscured by talus, or detrital materials, which have fallen from the Entrada above it, but the Carmel is readily visible at many places along the lake.

East of Rock Creek the red Entrada, capped by the thinnish Morrison Formation, rises above lake level and forms a portion of the striking cyclorama north of Dangling Rope, Driftwood Canyon, and Forbidding Canyon. Smaller, though by no means less beautiful, fragments of the Entrada are perched on the Carmel Formation along the outlying base of Navajo Mountain.

The base of Fiftymile Mountain, the eastern escarpment of the Kaiparowits Plateau, is visible northward from Dangling Rope, from where may be seen all of the formations listed above, from the Straight Cliffs Formation down to the Navajo Sandstone.

The formations continue to elevate eastward from Forbidding Canyon. The vertical massive cliffs at waterside are Navajo Sandstone, cross-bedded and sculpted in rounded forms with canyons cut vertically and with alcoves and grottos marking the canyon sides. Desert varnish and streaks of carbonaceous materials paint the surface with scenes of charm and splendor emphasized by the conchoidal scars of slab rock long since worn to dust and distributed to the Gulf of California.

A short distance from the mouth of Forbidding Canyon, in a tributary which drains the north slope of Navajo Mountain, a gigantic arch of stone bends gracefully over a narrow gorge from which flows a gentle trickle of clear water. The stone monument is a remnant of a slab of rock in a meander bend of the stream that flowed around the eastern edge of the slab. The waters cut away at both the upper and lower sides of the sandstone wall until a hole was produced, and the water flowed through this shortcut to the great river. This natural wonder was designated Rainbow Bridge. It is sculpted from the Navajo Sandstone which ornaments the northern base of Navajo Mountain like a clinging creature.

Near the confluence of the mighty San Juan with its graceful meanders, the Navajo Sandstone, too, rises above the lake level, and the bedded, maroon Kayenta Sandstone is revealed at the water's edge.

The Kayenta sits atop the most spectacular cliff-forming sandstone of them all, the Wingate. This formation shears off in tremendous rectangular blocks and forms almost vertical cliffs of great height. Only small portions of the Wingate are visible in the canyon of the Colorado between the confluence and the mouth of Escalante Canyon. The entire thickness of the Wingate is exposed in the vicinity of the Rincon. East along the San Juan River the Wingate rises above water level. Below it is the Chinle, a mass of varicolored muds and sandstones which are producers of uranium and which contain quantities of petrified wood. Beneath the Chinle is the maroon-to-red, purple, white, or green stratified muds of the Moenkopi Formation. Below the Moenkopi, still older formations are exposed along the uplifts eastward along the San Juan and northward along the Colorado, and the same or equivalent formations are present along the canyon of the Colorado southward from Lake Powell.

Reflections

The region is a difficult one for life. It is not passive (as some have suggested) but active in its relentlessness. One error of judgment might well be the last. Even those creatures which reside there, those to whom the region is home, are not immune to its dangers. One day during early September of 1971, a coyote lay on a talus slope between the shores of Lake Powell and the massive sandstone cliffs which stand wall-like back from the water's edge. The coyote was dead. We had witnessed its last few seconds of life. It had fallen from a narrow, gravelly ledge for more than a hundred feet in a gentle arc — almost as if in slow motion — while we gasped in horror and amazement and reached inwardly for some handhold. A wrong move on a ledge strewn with loose pebbles had cost the animal its life, and the day became a somber one for us. As we moved southward over the smooth surface of Lake Powell, we reflected upon the beauty of the scene, upon the harshness of this magnificent land, and upon the coincidence of the tragedy we had witnessed and the name of the canyon where it had happened — Last Chance.

Formidable are the cliffs, treacherous and forbidding to anyone traveling the area by land. Nearing the confluence of the Escalante River from the south, we are reminded that if one is sufficiently daring and well prepared, even this once remote region can be penetrated successfully. There is a narrow defile in the Navajo Sandstone on the west side of the canyon known as Hole-in-the-Rock, a crack in the cliff face where, unbelievably, wagonloads of Mormon men, women, and children with their livestock and gear lowered themselves into the depths of the inner gorge. Incredible enough was that feat, but it was not enough. They ascended the other side, traveling along pastel-pink canyon rims, anomalous in their appearance — for as soft as they look, they are as hard to climb as life itself was to endure for that hardy bunch. Months later, in April of 1880, they drew lots for home sites at Bluff along the San Juan River, not because that was where they were supposed to settle but because they were too tired to go further. The almost impossible trek from Escalante to Bluff had required the entire fall of 1879 and winter of 1880.

The Hole-in-the-Rock party traversed the region when the aridity of the land was not overwhelming, but even then the constant search for water troubled them. Thinking of the sufferings of the people of the

Hole-in-the-Rock expedition, we can consider it almost a crime to glide along the saran-wrap surface of Lake Powell in shaded comfort, sipping ice-water. Alongside, the rounded red rocks arise from purple depths; behind, crystal waters part in a wake of jewel-drops tumbling from a ridge of foam, where the propeller churns the water. "Out there" it is hot, searing hot and dry; a short hike of a few hundred yards is enough to desiccate a man and make him dizzy from heat — to make him wish for the cold waters of the nearby lake. The opposite is true, of course, when winter chills the air and the lake is abandoned by all save the hardy few, those who seek after solitude and the beauty of clear air and who at that season cannot bear to take the plunge into icy water.

One should try both the hike beneath the sun and the plunge into frigid waters. It seems almost a necessity for understanding the real grandeur of the place — the essence of this canyonland of slickrock country. Is this comfort of a man-made lake, this ease of travel, of reaching a "stark and wonderful land" a desecration? Shouldn't our travel here have been as difficult as that of the Hole-in-the-Rock party, or at least as difficult as that of those in the Powell expedition of 1869 who floated here some hundreds of feet below where we now glide? Surely, the people of the Hole-in-the-Rock would have no such thoughts — not after months of grueling labor, of sweat and tears for each wearing step. One must suffer somewhat in order to enjoy what is good in life; pain allows you to know that you have lived.

It is that kind of country — this slickrock land — the kind that puts conflicting thoughts in your head and disturbing emotions inside you. The land is no doubt a harsh one: heat and cold, drought and flood, wind and calm, starvation and plenty, life and death. No matter what happens, it happens in large doses. It is a land of pink, rounded forms appearing as soft as a baby's skin, of pastels of land and rocks and flower blossoms, of azure skies hung with rainbows after a violent storm of summer when eerie white clouds creep out of the gray and over the cliffs to skim down into the canyons. It is a huge, empty, lonely land, enduring, it would seem, everything, even the intrusion of Lake Powell, its massive waters burying for an eternity the innermost secrets of that deep canyonland. Indeed, it ignores us who dare broach the void of time and space. We are passengers on a doomed inland sea of exquisite beauty.

Emotions aroused by experiencing the lake are difficult to pass off lightly: the poignancy after a rainstorm when curtains of water spill in lacy torrents over a cliff face, the exultation when waterfalls roar and thunder and splash into the lake, the yearning when the early morning air is crystal amber and the sun pours lemon shades over the rocks and lake or when sandstone glows salmon under the waning moon, quarter full in the western sky. Perhaps (but it is hard to say) the fascination of the region reaches us most of all on a midnight when the landscape is ethereal and the full moon's light dapples the surface of the lake and bathes the cliffs in silver shrouds, emphasizing the mysterious black of nighttime shadows.

The paradox involves a conflict between that which is, the present real world, and that which was or might have been. To experience it as it is brings sheer delight; to contemplate that which was is bittersweet. So it goes, this contemplation of charm and violence, of magnificence and disaster, of black waters and blue sky against a cyclorama of time — Lake Powell.

Left: Gateway to a land of strange-sounding names — Wahweap, Warm Creek, Last Chance, Four Mile, Paradise, Iceburg, Aztec, and Hidden Passage — this land of arid desolation calls out to be understood.

Below left: Waters of tributaries of the mighty Colorado have cut grand-scale sculptures laterally from the main channel of the river; cubic miles of materials have gone down the rivers. Here, the Muddy River of the San Rafael Swell is entrenched through the Moenkopi and into the Kaibab Limestone of the Grand Canyon sequence of formations.

Below: Monuments at the edges of the great valley represent mere remnants of formations that were once continuous across the canyon of the Colorado. Capped by a protective layer of resistant stone, the monuments resist, for a while, the aggressive and persistent agents of erosion. North Cainville Mesa stands as a reminder of the interaction of wind and water with stone of differing degrees of hardness.

28

Left: Gray on gray becomes a play of yellow on brown and black in the afternoon sun. The great monuments known as Factory Butte and North Cainville Mesa rise from the horizontal bedding and erosional plain of the central western portion of the Navajo Basin.

Above: Elevated by intrusive volcanics, the mountains within the Navajo Basin are marked by erosion. Planes of deposition of sedimentary strata slope gently, then steeply, up the flanks of the volcanic rocks at the core of Mt. Hillers in the Henry Mountains.

Left: Plateau country in the southwestern quadrant of the basin is dominated by the elevated Straight Cliffs portion of Fiftymile Mountain of the Kaiparowits Plateau. The view east from Fiftymile Point shows the erosional features of the lands in the vicinity of the confluence of the San Juan and Glen Canyons of the Colorado.

Below: South from Fiftymile Point the benchlands drop quickly to the buttressed bases of Entrada Sandstone along the east side of Twilight Canyon, and Navajo Mountain, great, unbroached, laccolithic, dominates the southern reaches of Glen Canyon.

Left: Fiftymile Mountain, viewed from the summit of Navajo Mountain, stands tablelike, forming a vast barrier that stretches more than fifty miles southeastward from Escalante. Benchlands mark the less resistant strata and cliffs the more resistant ones. Clad in juniper and pinyon woodland, the Straight Cliffs formation atop the plateau is the youngest. Downward to the waters' edge the age of the formations increases. The formations are Tropic Shale (bench), Morrison and Entrada (cliff), Carmel (thin, but forming a broad bench), and Navajo (canyon cliffs at lakeside).

Below: East from Escalante and Boulder and west from the Henry Mountains is a peculiar bulge of rocks, marked with deeply entrenched, water-bearing canyons and water-filled erosional basins, known as the Waterpocket Fold. Strata ages younger than Navajo Sandstone are missing, having been worn away completely. At the northern end of the Fold the cliff-forming sandstones arch around the base of Boulder Mountain and form the Circle Cliffs region. Canyons are cut below the white sands of the Navajo, through the platy strata of the Kayenta and massive Wingate, to the less resistant silty layers of the Chinle formation.

The eastern flank of the Waterpocket Fold plunges steeply, with the formations reappearing along the flanks of the Henry Mountains to the east. Thus, the layered geology is read like pages of a book though not so easily because the formations change in color, texture, and substance from one place to another, depending upon the conditions of their origin. Or the formation thins and disappears, placing in context two formations that are separated elsewhere.

Left: Southward, the axis of Waterpocket Fold lowers in elevation. Long ago, near the southern end, the river had become entrenched in a graceful meander centered in the Fold. Finally, the river wore away the median of the meander and broached it, leaving the meander bed abandoned. Thus, the Rincon, fringed with Kayenta and Wingate Sandstones and layered with drifting sands over the Chinle and upper Moenkopi, was formed.

Below Left: The arc of Waterpocket Fold, capped in this southern extension with the Kayenta, a resistant platform protecting underlying formations and supporting others, seems to bear the peaks of the Henries miles distant from the Rincon. Soft layers of Chinle and Moenkopi absorb water slowly and liquify, flowing into the channel that is beneath Lake Powell. As these supporting formations give way and sink, they carry the cliffs of sandstone into the lake with them. Massive avalanches and the premature filling of Lake Powell result.

Below: East of Waterpocket Fold a broad and gentle valley has been eroded to the Navajo slickrock of drainage-patterned and sand-pocketed stone, capped in some places by benches of Carmel formation covered with blackbrush. Atop this in the Bullfrog-Hall's Crossing vicinity lie the rounded reddish hills of Entrada Sandstone. Bays of Lake Powell fill the sloping basins.

Left: To the west of the Kaiparowits Plateau proper is the Cockscomb, a result of the plunging east flank of the East Kaibab monocline. Navajo, Carmel, Entrada, Tropic Shale, and Straight Cliffs formations form a series of strike valleys, hogbacks, and cuestas, which form the Cockscomb. Splendid remnants of formations produced by weathering form a "jewelbox" at the head of Cottonwood wash.

Below: West of the Cockscomb the formations and their remains level out, with the massive sandstones forming the White Cliffs escarpment. Here, Calico Peak, a cone-shaped portion of Navajo, rests atop the plateau. Because the weathered surface of the plain and the underlying rocks do not erode at the same rate, some portions are rounded in haystack form, the similiarity made the more striking because of the variegated sands of the formations.

Above: The Kaiparowits Plateau consists of formations dipping northward, and in the south flank of these formations are the streams that drain the plateau. Between the canyons of the south flank are benchlands terminating in castellated buttes, towers, and figures. At the south end of Smoky Mountain benchland is a butte called "None," having no official designation. Here, None Butte is contrasted in the snows of a day in winter.

Right: Upstream a few miles from Lee's Ferry, a site visited by both John Wesley Powell and members of the Escalante-Dominguez party, is Glen Canyon Dam — a monument to modern technology. Constructed at great cost, the dam effectively stopped the flow of the river and turned the inner gorge of Glen Canyon into a huge lake, named to honor Powell. Mirrored in its surface are the clouds of a winter day, and back from the edge stand the stacks of industry, made possible by the water of the lake.

Sky repeated in reflection in Warm Creek Bay, along with distant monoliths and imposing Navajo Mountain, give impressions of vast space — overwhelming and almost unreal.

Left: The tops of monoliths separate and move toward one, mirrored in leaden-silver and copper-colored waters of Padre Bay.

Below: Water tends to compliment its setting. Rather than distracting from the surroundings, water adds greatly to the scene; even muddied waters viewed from a proper angle mirror the land alongside, doubling the images. Here the quiet, clear water on a day in early spring mirrors some monoliths at Padre Point.

Left: Around a bend the mirrored surface gives way to troubled waters, dimpled at first, then sullen and rugged, with snow-capped waves. The smooth, swishing sound of water pouring from the keel of the boat changes to the staccato of rapid-fire gunnery, and finally to the clap of surf-pounded waves.

Above: The scene changes, not only with the passage of time or with changing light, but with one's perception of it. If he truly perceives a scene, he captures it and it is his, stored either in his conscious or his subconscious, to be remembered again at some quiet moment. Here is a peculiar quality of water near Tower Butte on a winter day.

Kind of light, transparency of air, shape and number of clouds, proportion of blue sky, shadows, red rock, and the surface of this tranquil, man-made sea combine to provide a scene of charm and delight at Gunsight Butte in the spring.

Left: Gates of some familiar passage open, as if doors had been pushed aside, as if a bright new world had been created *de novo,* yielding a view of wave-lapped lake, monuments in silhouette, threatening sky, and evidence of a dying sun. The view, west from Last Chance Bay on an evening in autumn, can be either savored or ignored.

Above: Southward from the lake, on a platform of Navajo Sandstone, stand the impressive monuments of the Rainbow Plateau. Carved in Entrada Sandstone and sometimes capped with a resistant member of the Morrison formation, these figures in stone are underlaid by the thin Carmel formation of mud or siltstone that controls the retreat of the cliffs of more resistant stone.

Long, filtered rays of red light from a setting sun cast long shadows from the monoliths west from Last Chance Bay, intensifying the redness of stone.

Below: A waning moon lingers in the western sky, adding its feeble light to the brilliance of a morning sun. Tranquil waters reflect the orange-red sandstone of Gunsight Butte, modified in color by the red rays of the rising sun.

Right: Leaden skies and leaden water mark a sullen day in winter, while the wake, churned white by a revolving propellor, points at a boat. Snow-layered summits, black and gray on white, present an aspect seemingly alien to a land where skies of blue and heat of summer days most often greet the traveler along the straightaway southwest from Rock Creek Bay.

Below Right: Trenchlike, the inner gorge of Glen Canyon, now filled by Lake Powell, is bounded by towering walls formed by the Morrison, Entrada, and Carmel escarpment. Eastward from Cathedral and Driftwood canyons, the Navajo Sandstone rises gently, forming massive cliffs at waterside.

Left: In early springtime and later winter, storms of a cyclonic nature sweep southward to the Lake Powell vicinity. Some are gentle, producing a windless patter of raindrops on land and canvas, but others are accompanied by strong and violent winds, which react in peculiar manner in the canyons and on the lake. Tents are flattened, boats are filled with water, and travelers are treated to alarming discomfort. The stone and sand take on an entirely different appearance when wet, as here at the confluence of the San Juan in late winter.

Below: Formidable is the land; a gigantic platform of Navajo Sandstone is dissected by tributaries of the magnificent Colorado River, whose gorge is the greatest natural obstacle in the region. Here, at Hole-in-the-Rock, on the western side of the platform, and in Cottonwood Canyon, in the foreground, a group of pioneers made a valiant effort in December of 1879 and January of 1880. A road was constructed through the seemingly impassible "hole," then eastward up the valley of Cottonwood Canyon.

Above Left: Reflections are reproduced in inverted form, and one gets a "standing on one's head" view of the world of water, rock, and sky. In undulating surfaces the inversion tends to form a surrealistic view, moving in graceful, ever-changing, dreamlike forms, as here in Reflection Canyon on an autumn evening.

Above: Canyon walls are seldom straight or even gently curving. Rather, they are made of a series of meander bends whose spurs once made of the stream bed a serpentine pattern with s- and z-shaped curves. Death-still calm allows for reproduction of remains of meander spurs in mirrored image on a morning in Reflection Canyon in winter.

Left: Adding charm and grace even in death, the naked twigs and dark trunk of a drowned Fremont cottonwood is repeated in the almost invisible surface of the water before a gigantic alcove in Navajo Sandstone in Reflection Canyon on a winter day.

Below: Glassy stillness allows the perception of stone and water in a kaleidoscopic sequence. Except for more intense colors of stone and sky, the image in water almost exactly repeats the actual scene in Forbidding Canyon at the entrance to Rainbow Marina.

Right: Dimpled surfaces in a shaded bay in afternoon provide a play in color on the sunlit stone eastward. In a soothing calmness that induces relaxation and contemplation, the action of light on water is pleasing.

Below right: Massive though the stone of the canyon sides actually is, it is not of uniform texture or solidity. The strata have been subjected to tremendous forces, and cracks, known as joints, have been formed that penetrate deep into the strata or entirely through them. These joints are seen in aerial view as a reticulate pattern on the surface of the stone. The joints are more easily eroded than areas between them. Here, at the haystack bend south from Cottonwood Canyon, mounds of rock alternate with joints at nearly right angles to the canyon wall.

Left: Hole-in-the-Rock, where wagonloads of Mormon men, women, and children with their livestock and gear inched to the bottom of the gorge through a crack in this cliff face. Later, they traveled pink canyon rims, soft looking but as hard to pass over as life itself was for that hardy group.

Below: Shadows cast by cliffs in the morning sun darken cliffs, alcoves, and breeze-roughened water. Breezes sweep the water, north from near the confluence of the San Juan.

Left: Midday light is more direct than light in morning or evening, and the reddish hues of those longer rays are subdued at midday. Red stone turns to buff marked with brown of desert varnish. A combination of form and shadow on textured stone and rippled water spells intrigue at the Three Garden reentry on a day in March.

Below: Falling slabs of stone frequently break to the great fractures or joints in the rock, leaving columns or pillars of monumental size and form. Appearing almost architectural, the great height of these impressive vertical structures is enhanced by their apparent continuation in the mirrored surface of the water west from Cottonwood Canyon on a morning in March.

Left: Canyons of awe, charm, and intrigue depart from lands adjacent to the lake. Carved out of stone, the canyons often contain streams of clear water that flows from the porous rock. Persistence of the tiny perennial stream and of the intense storm-induced torrents that occur irregularly have caused the channel to become entrenched in graceful chasms. Water for drinking or for a bath is available in Aztec Canyon on a morning in February.

Above: Here, too, water in a shallow pool adds to the setting; the rock seems to bleed with color. Delightful in any season, Aztec Canyon on a winter day provides an interlude of silence and dwarfing panoramas.

Left: Straight lines in nature occur with sufficient regularity to break the rounded and curving lines of irregularly patterned scenery. Crystal water over rounded cobble depicts a motif not often encountered in the canyons of the region. This small opening in the otherwise narrow chasm that is Aztec Canyon allows a breathing point in an otherwise breathless traverse of a splendid canyon.

Below: Generally reddish to buff, some portions of the gigantic Navajo Sandstone are colored in other shades. Basic texture remains the same, cross-bedded dunes in stone, but water action cuts it more easily here, less easily there, producing irregularly rounded, cavernous channels. The gentle trickle of water fills the channels, and unless windswept they mirror the upper walls of the narrow gorge that is Aztec Canyon.

Left: Glaze of desert varnish — oxides of magnesium — reflects as burnished copper and gives a quality of light unseen in duller surfaces. Water-washed stain of black-brown indicates where centuries of rains have moistened the protected underside of an overhanging wall in Aztec Canyon.

Above: Prince's Plume (*Stanleya pinnata* [Pursh] Britt.) flowers in profusion on the siltstone of the Cutler formation at Hite.

Left: Boulders of Wingate Sandstone adorn a beach of Chinle mudstone at Piute Canyon along the San Juan arm. Mudstones and siltstones such as this are unstable when wet, and here also the formations ooze gradually lakeward. Massive landslides have already sunk previous landmarks into the lake, filling the basin with sediment not carried in by entering streams.

Above: Slabs of rock fall from stone cliffs and persist for a while on the canyon slopes or in the bottoms. Gradually, they are acted on by wind, water, and differential heating and cooling. Grain by grain they are worn away, and the particles are swept away by still more wind and water. That the processes of erosion about equal the rate of rock fall is demonstrated by the paucity of such boulders. Otherwise, the canyons would be choked by their remains. San Juan arm and other canyons of the Colorado bear the reminders of processes of canyon formation.

Above: Slickrock offers little to control the flow of water from even gentle rains. When the surface has become wet, the water cascades from the stone, first as thin layers that collect in tiny depressions and finally as bounding waterfalls that pour over cliffs into plunge basins or into the lake below.

Right: Remnant of a meander spur, Navajo Bridge, is a slender arc of stone spanning a shallow canyon cut into the Kayenta Sandstone platform. Evidence of the former existence of the stream-carved channel around the east end of the span is clearly seen in the curved alcove at the base of the canyon wall. Ages of water-flow cut away the stone until the slender spur was worn through; then the water followed the shortcut under the bridge toward Forbidding Canyon proper.

Left: In a view never to be seen again by those now living, the canyon beneath the bridge is here clothed by brown-yellow grasses in winter dormancy. Rising waters of the lake have obliterated the vegetation, and the ring of water-soaked and dried stone replaces the living plants. This will continue, since the lake draw-down will maintain the ring of stained stone.

Below: Each attempt at progress in a civilization represents a trade-off, and Lake Powell is no exception. For electrical energy, recreation of the masses, labor for construction workers and others, a canyon of intrigue, a vegetative assembly unlike that anywhere, and the charm and beauty of places known and unknown became the pawns in the trade.

Above left: On a clear day, when one is in an aircraft at a very high elevation, it is possible to see the length of the state of Utah and to discern Navajo Mountain, a landmark on the southern horizon. It stands above Lake Powell, changing its face from hour to hour, from day to day, and from season to season. Crowned with forest and wearing, skirtlike, the remnants of massive sandstones along its base, the mountain is cool in summer and snowcapped in winter.

Above: Extending serpentlike in Glen Canyon, Lake Powell angles to the southwest toward the confluence of the San Juan. Brooding Navajo Mountain stands above the lake, seemingly perched atop the Rainbow Plateau. Normally imposing, the mountain becomes even more impressive in summer when clouds cap the summit from air upwelling along its slopes. Rainfall on the mountain is greater than in the low elevations surrounding it and accounts for the forests on the higher slopes.

Left: Vegetated alcoves, the glens of Glen Canyon, are numerous in the Navajo Sandstone bordering the lake. In size, these alcoves vary greatly. They are usually associated with moist bedding planes in the stone, where water reaches the edge of a canyon wall. Seeds and spores of plants germinate on the moistened surface, and grow to form hanging gardens.

Left: Gentle curves in stone, blue-black water, and cloud-flocked sky combine to form an impressive sight. Alcoves occur along planes at several levels in the canyon walls, changing the character of the stone. Sheer straight walls offer spectacular sights here and there in the canyons along the lake, but those sculpted into rounded forms and dimpled with alcoves provide charm to the variation that is the canyon side.

Above: Not only is it possible to experience serendipity at Lake Powell, it is also possible to prove the existence of it. An unexpected discovery of form in stone, a curving shore line, and the play of afternoon light is captured by the closing of a shutter, the entire scene to be experienced again later, as demonstrated in this view west from near the confluence.

Above: Oak glens are modern hanging gardens, and they occur in two main types. The type featured here has a flat face wall corresponding to a joint surface. The vaulted arch stands high above the vegetated portion of this window-blind type of garden near the confluence. Water reaches the garden along the fractures in the sandstone, providing moisture on a continuous basis in this land that is perpetually short of water. Trees and other water-loving plants cluster about the life-giving moisture in Willow Garden.

Right: Classic alcoves formed along moist bedding planes constitute the most common type of hanging garden. It is in this type that the most peculiar assemblages of vegetation surrounding moist sites occur. Often the occurrence of an alcove is associated with drainage in the sandstone above them, and downpours cascade over the lip of the stone above the alcove. Waterfalls drop to the next level and finally reach Lake Powell, where their energy is dissipated.

Left: Stone along the drainages slows the water from intense storms, but not uniformly. It swirls over the surface, curved by excessive drag, and thus carves the stone irregularly. Swirl holes are worn in the sloping channel, retaining water long after the completion of the storm that filled them and providing habitats for numerous aquatic animals and plants.

Above: In springtime and early summer, following downpours, the canyon tree frog, *Hyla arenicolor* (pictured here), and the red-spotted toad, *Bufo punctatus,* congregate at the pools in stone basins. At sunset the first aspirant of the frog-toad group in the seasonal throb of life begins to sing, a trill or a blat depending on the species. Silence follows, sometimes broken by the gentle and plaintive call of the canyon wren. Then the frog or toad calls again. Soon it is joined by another player, and another, until an entire amorous chorus reaches a cacophonous crescendo, echoed by the cliffs nearby. In morning all is silent as the singers sleep in a peaceful, mud-coated, semi-aquatic world.

Above: Alcoves vary in size and form from minute to gigantic. Viewed from a distance, the scale is deceiving; the alcove is best experienced close up. When one is dwarfed by an alcove of sufficient dimensions to house full-grown trees, lush vegetation, gushing streams issuing from stone, and great slopes of sand and broken rock, the real size of the alcove is apparent. Such an alcove is the one designated here as Death Camas Garden in the first meander of the San Juan arm east of the confluence.

Right: A hike into any of the canyons carved into Navajo Sandstone is likely to reveal one or more hanging gardens. Each is different in some way; yet there is a sameness too. Differing in size and shape, they house many of the species common to gardens in the vicinity. The alcoves provide cooling shade on a hot day in summer and protection from downpours or cold winds in winter. A set of gardens in paired classic alcoves is situated in the canyon north of the first meander of the San Juan arm east of the confluence.

Left: Pools of water exist in at least some of the hanging gardens. Often these are the plunge basins formed by waterfalls from overhanging cliffs. Prior to the existence of the lake, these were sources of clear, cool water to passersby — animals or humans. Rising waters of the lake have flooded this magnificent pool and its fringe of sawgrass, *Cladium californicum*. This pool and its mantle of vegetation witnessed a last springtime and then was drowned.

Below: Sawgrass (*Cladium californicum*) is a plant of generally warmer climes than at Glen Canyon's; yet it has survived here for centuries, evidenced by several feet of sawgrass remains in some sites at Lake Powell. That it is more typical of torrid habitats is indicated by its presence in Death Valley, along Furnace Creek. The known habitats of this species in Utah are now slowly disappearing beneath the surface of the lake.

Left: A final springtime came for the garden that we named Cladium. Cladium garden was situated in a narrow alcove in the first meander in Hidden Passage Canyon. A shelf of gently sloping stone allowed one access from the east side, and there driftwood congregated. Now, the shelf, the garden, and the driftwood are gone, only the latter to reappear in the valleys of a wave-patterned plain.

Above: Light of a May morning shows the fresh green of maidenhair fern in a shaded glen. Flowing water from an alcove dampens the drainage bottom and soaks into the sandy margins. Trees provide cooling shade where travelers have for years been lured to Contrary Gardens, north of the confluence.

   Left: Five hundred feet of stone tower above the stream bottoms in some canyons along the side of Lake Powell. Gigantic falls pour from the margins of alcoves when storms flood the watersheds at the heads of the canyons. Plunge basins and stream channels, both lined with dense stands of vegetation, are characteristic of the canyons. Here, cattail forms a stand against a backdrop of other plants and the box end of a tributary to Escalante Canyon.
   Above: Plants of the Lake Powell region are adapted for survival in a limited number of habitats. Because of plant specialization, a mosaic of vegetative types is formed. The heleborine orchid is confined mainly to the hanging gardens in canyons along the lake. Here it is presented, in fruit, with a background of a dry garden in a late afternoon.

Left: Cardinal flower, *Lobelia cardinalis,* is widespread in the eastern and southern states. It reaches its northernmost limits in Utah in the Lake Powell vicintity, growing in some hanging gardens and along the channels draining from them. The brilliant red of the cardinal flower is an unusual flower color in the region.

Below: Perhaps the most unique species of plants in the hanging gardens are the clingers — those that grow attached to the vertical or overhanging stone walls in alcoves; some of these plant species are almost entirely restricted to the gardens. The cave primrose, *Primula specuicola,* is one of the unusual plants restricted to hanging gardens. It is known only from the vicinity of the Colorado Plateau.

Left: When evening comes to the canyons along Lake Powell during summer, the bright yellow flowers of the long-tubed evening-primrose, *Oenothera longissima,* open their petals in a wide-faced display of magnificent symmetry. Dangling cobwebby strands of pollen adhere to the anthers and cloak the night visitors who harvest nectar. In morning the flowers close, obscuring their beauty from the light of day.

Below: Burros, *Equus asinus,* dwell in the arid lands south of Lake Powell. Curious and sure-footed, they eye the visitor to the lake with a clear knowledge of how to tantilize and yet avoid pursuit and capture. They seem to perceive the distance that provides the margin of safety, and the visitor can approach only to that point. When he reaches it, the burros retreat and await the approach again.

Left: The splashing plop of a leopard frog in a plunge basin pool reminds one that here is a diurnal amphibian to balance the nocturnal ones that sing and perform in the dim light of evening. Graceful and colorfully marked, the leopard frog leaps into the water in a sweeping arc; then with a kick of its sturdy legs, the frog disappears in the depths of the pond. Finally, it reappears, alligator-like, with only its eyes protruding.

Above: Birds of many kinds visit the gardens, but few really inhabit them. Wrens and sparrows are the most common inhabitants; others are mainly itinerants who find the gardens convenient. Owls sometimes nest on a shelf high in an alcove, using the rock face as a nest site in late winter and early spring. The fledglings are ready to fly before spring gives way to summer. Here, a young great horned owl rests on a shelf near an alcove.

Left: Cacti of several types grow on the sandy terraces and benchlands in the region. The most bizzare of these is the small barrel-shaped fishhook cactus, *Sclerocactus whipplei,* whose hooked spines effectively protect it from most grazing enemies. Flowers crown the summit of the green stem in springtime.

Below left: Moon lily, sacred datura, and jimsonweed are among the many names given to this poisonous plant, whose flowers are the largest of any in the region. The plant, *Datura meteloides,* is grayish-green and has an odor similar to that of a wet dog. The flowers, however, are sweetly scented, and can be seven or more inches long and sometimes more than five inches broad. Opening in evening, they are pollinated by moths, which reach the nectaries deep within the flowers.

Below: Even in fruit the western redbud, *Cersis occidentalis,* adds beauty to the alcoves and bottoms of wet canyons in the region. The pink blossoms appear as the leaves unfold in April and May. Much of the habitat available in Utah for this lovely plant is now inundated.

Above left: Drifting sands on some benchlands are occupied by plants capable of tolerating the ever-moving substrata. One of these, the pale evening-primrose, *Oenothera pallida,* is superbly adapted.

Left: So remote was the canyon of the Colorado, and so difficult was the collection of plants by the few botanists who visited the canyon, that several species remained unnamed and undescribed. This was the case with the Toft yucca, *Yucca toftiae,* which was collected by the writers along the margin of the lake.

Above: Early maps of the Glen Canyon show forested bars and terraces along the river, deep in its canyon. Few trees remain in the side canyons as reminders of those dead and gone from the margins of the buried river channel. An example of the type is this gnarled monument to time, a Fremont poplar, *Populus fremontii,* pictured here above the level of the lake at the head of Cataract Canyon.

Black shadows and shades of blue silhouette the features on the northwest side of Gregory Butte, which stands resolutely south from a bay called Last Chance. Their features characterize the paradox that is Lake Powell, startling beauty masking a drowned world, a world destroyed — unknown and unknowable.